THE MYSTERY OF ALLEGRA

She is five years and three months old. She wears a long white nightdress and she has blond hair and big eyes, as blue as an Italian sky in summer. Her voice is soft and sweet, and she wants Adrian to take her to her Mamà, who is a long way away.

Adrian is on holiday, travelling in Italy with his parents. Late one evening they find the Villa Henderson and decide to take rooms there for the night. But Adrian wakes in the middle of the night to find Allegra in his room, with her big blue eyes and cold little hands. At first Adrian is very surprised, then he remembers that Chiara Henderson said she had a little daughter. But why does Allegra say that her mother is a long way away? And Adrian's bedroom door is locked, so how did Allegra get into his room?

Adrian does not understand. He decides to ask Allegra's mother in the morning. But in the morning he has a very big surprise . . .

OXFORD BOOKWORMS LIBRARY

Fantasy & Horror

The Mystery of Allegra

Stage 2 (700 headwords)

Series Editor: Jennifer Bassett
Founder Editor: Tricia Hedge
Activities Editors: Jennifer Bassett and Alison Baxter

PETER FOREMAN

The Mystery of
Allegra

OXFORD UNIVERSITY PRESS

OXFORD
UNIVERSITY PRESS

Great Clarendon Street, Oxford, OX2 6DP, United Kingdom

Oxford University Press is a department of the University of Oxford.
It furthers the University's objective of excellence in research, scholarship,
and education by publishing worldwide. Oxford is a registered trade
mark of Oxford University Press in the UK and in certain other countries

ISBN: 978 0 19 479066 6   Book
ISBN: 978 0 19 463766 4   Book and audio pack

Printed in China

Word count (main text): 6,115 words

For more information on the Oxford Bookworms Library,
visit www.oup.com/elt/gradedreaders

ACKNOWLEDGEMENTS
Illustrated by Jenny Brackley
Cover image by Abdul Kadir Audah

CONTENTS

1
Allegra One

I met Allegra one night in April twelve years ago. I was sixteen years old and she was only five.

I remember that it rained a lot that night and we arrived late at the house. We were driving along a dark road when my mother saw a sign, which said in big letters: *Villa Henderson – Bed and Breakfast.*

'It's in English!' my mother said. She was surprised because we were on holiday in Italy.

My father turned right and drove along an old road. When we arrived, we saw a big villa with tall black trees around it. There was a light in one of the windows, and on the wall above the door were the words *Villa Henderson.*

My father knocked at the door and a small woman opened it. She was about sixty and wore strange clothes.

'Are you English?' my father asked.

'Yes, I am,' she answered in a quiet voice.

'We're looking for rooms for the night. Can we stay here?'

'Please come in.'

We went into a long, comfortable room. There was a bright fire in the old fire-place, which gave a beautiful, warm light.

'The weather is very bad,' said the woman. 'It's cold for April. I'll make some tea for you.'

When she went out, we looked around the room. There were lots of English tables and chairs in dark wood, and the walls and floor were of stone. There were two big armchairs in front of the fire and a large black dog was sleeping in one of them.

'I like this room,' said my mother. 'It looks comfortable, but it's beautiful too.'

Just then the woman returned with the tea. Behind her came a woman in a long black dress.

Behind her came a woman in a long black dress.

'My name is Margaret Henderson,' said the old woman, 'and this is my daughter Chiara. She has a daughter too, so I'm a grandmother.'

'My daughter is in bed,' smiled Chiara.

She was a tall woman, with long, fair hair and blue eyes. She was perhaps about thirty-five.

'Have you come far today?' she asked.

'Yes,' my father replied. 'We're very tired.'

'Your rooms are ready for you. I'll take you up when you've had your tea.'

So, after tea, we went up some stairs and followed Chiara along a corridor. She stopped at a door and told my parents that it was their room. Then she looked at me.

'Your room is round the corner. Come this way, please.'

We turned right and walked along another corridor. My room was at the end.

'Good night and sleep well,' said Chiara with a smile.

But I didn't sleep well.

I locked the door and after five minutes I was in bed. The house was silent, but I could hear the rain on the window and the strong wind in the trees outside. I slept a little, woke up, then slept again. And then I woke up suddenly. The window shutters were making a loud noise against the wall. I could see that the window was open because the long white curtains were moving in the wind. I got up and closed both the shutters and the

3

window. Now the room was very dark, so I walked with my hands out in front of me, to try and find the light on the table by the bed. My left hand touched the table – and then something took hold of my right arm.

It was a cold little hand. The hair on my neck stood up and my legs began to shake.

'Who is it?' I cried.

At the same time I found the light on the table and turned it on. A little girl in a long white nightdress stood in front of me near the bed. She was looking at me with big eyes, as blue as an Italian sky in summer. Her blond hair was as bright as sunlight round her pale face.

'What a beautiful child!' I thought.

'Hallo. My name's Allegra,' she said.

Her voice was soft and sweet and she spoke English beautifully. But she couldn't say the letter 'r'.

'Did you come in through the window?' I asked.

But she answered me with a question. 'What's your name?'

'Adrian.'

'I'm five years and three months old,' she said. 'How old are you?'

'Sixteen. How did you get in here?'

'Don't be angry with me, Adrian,' she said.

'I'm not angry with you. Don't cry. Tell me your name again.'

'What a beautiful child!' I thought.

'Allegra. It means happy in Italian.'

'What are you doing here, Allegra? What do you want?'

'Will you take me to my Mamà?' she asked suddenly.

I looked at her in surprise. 'But you know where your mother is,' I said.

'Yes, but she's a long way from here.'

'No, she isn't, Allegra. She's in this house.'

'I want to see Mamà. Will you take me, please?'

'No, Allegra. She'll be angry with you because you aren't in bed.'

'Oh no, Mamà was never angry with me,' she said with a little smile. 'But sometimes Papà was angry and I was afraid of him.'

For a while I didn't speak, and I just looked at her. Why did she say 'was' and not 'is' when she spoke about her parents? She was a very strange little girl.

'You must go back to bed now, Allegra,' I said. 'I'm not going to take you to your mother.'

She looked at me, and now her blue eyes were sad.

'Will you take me to Mamà tomorrow then?'

'Yes.'

'Oh, thank you!' she cried happily.

'Now, where is your room?'

'It's next to this one.'

'Okay, let's go.'

And I took her hand, her cold little hand. Just then the window opened again and the wind and rain came in. I went to the window to close it but the curtains flew up in my face and I couldn't see anything. I closed the window. And when I turned round, Allegra wasn't there.

For a minute I just stood still. Then I unlocked my door and went along the corridor. There was a door on the left. I opened it slowly. The room was dark but

I could see that it was a child's room. Somebody was sleeping in a bed near the window.

'Good!' I thought. 'She's in bed now.' And I closed the door.

Next morning, after breakfast, we went into the garden. There were beautiful hills and woods around it. I walked round to the back of the house because I wanted to look

Someone was sleeping in a bed near the window.

7

at the windows of my room and Allegra's room. There was a big tree between them near the wall of the house.

'Perhaps she got out of her window on to the tree, and then got in through my window,' I thought. But it looked a difficult and dangerous thing to do. Possible for an adult perhaps, but not for a girl of five.

When I went back to the front garden, Allegra's mother was there. She was talking to my parents.

'Did your shutters open last night?' she asked. 'I heard a noise.'

'No,' replied my mother. 'But we heard a noise too.'

'It was the shutters in my room,' I said.

'Oh, I'm sorry,' said Chiara. 'Those shutters are very old. But I hope you slept well after you closed them.'

'Shall I tell her?' I thought. Then I said with a smile, 'Yes, I slept well, thank you – but only after your daughter's visit.'

'Allegra?' Chiara was very surprised.

'Yes, she came to my room in the middle of the night.'

'Did she? Well, I know she sometimes walks in her sleep.'

'But . . .' I began. And I stopped. Again I thought: 'Shall I tell her?'

But I decided not to say that the door was locked. I knew they wouldn't believe me, and I thought that they would laugh at me. So I just said that Allegra was a beautiful child.

'Yes, she is,' Chiara answered. 'But she isn't a very happy girl.'

'Doesn't her name mean happy in Italian?'

'Yes, but I've never met an Italian child called Allegra.'

'Why did you call her Allegra?' my mother asked.

'I don't know. The name came to me suddenly. Perhaps I wanted a happy child.' And Chiara smiled sadly.

Then she turned to the house and called her daughter.

'Allegra! Come downstairs, please!'

'I'm coming!' came a shout from the house.

We heard Allegra on the stairs; then she came out. I looked at her. I looked and looked. But I couldn't believe my eyes.

2
Allegra Two

She was pale and beautiful, like the girl in my room. But this was a different girl. This Allegra had long black hair and her eyes were brown.

'Hallo,' she said.

Was it the same voice? It was soft and sweet but – I wasn't sure!

'This is Adrian,' said Chiara. 'He says that you went into his room last night, Allegra.'

This was a different girl.

The girl looked at me in surprise.

'No, Mummy, I wasn't in his room.' She spoke English beautifully, but she couldn't say the letter 'r'!

'You see, she doesn't remember,' Chiara said to me. 'I think that she was walking in her sleep again.'

When I went to bed that night, I couldn't sleep. I was waiting for the girl and I was afraid. But after about an hour my eyes closed and I slept. I woke up suddenly when a cold little hand touched my face. The girl's voice spoke softly in my ear.

'Wake up, Adrian, wake up . . .'

I turned on the light. She was there; but was she real? Her skin was like milk, her blond hair was like sunlight in the room. She was wearing the long, white nightdress.

'Is she real or is this a dream?' I thought.

And I touched her face. It was cold, very cold. But it was real.

'Will you take me to Mamà now?' she asked.

I looked at the window. It was closed. Then I went to the door. It was locked. I began to feel very afraid.

'How did you get in here?' I asked.

'You weren't here so I waited for you. I was sleeping behind that curtain.'

She showed me a curtain in a corner of the room. There was another, smaller bed for a child behind it. So she was in the room before I came! But where did she come from, and who was her mother?

'Okay, I'll take you to your mother,' I said. 'Where is she?'

Suddenly the girl began to speak in Italian. 'She's at Bagno a Ripoli, near Florence.'

'But we can't go to Florence tonight!' I said. I could understand Italian, but I spoke in English.

'You *must* take me!' Allegra said angrily, speaking in English again. 'I want to see my Mamà tonight. I want to see her before I die.' Then she began to cry.

Die! What did she mean?

'Why do you say that?' I said in surprise. 'You're not going to die.'

'Yes, I am. I know, I know! Papà didn't like Mamà and he took me away from her. I didn't see her for a long time. I wanted to see her and she wanted to see me too. Oh, I must see her before I die!'

Again I couldn't understand why she spoke in the past. I really couldn't understand anything! Was this all a little girl's fantasy? I decided to ask her some questions.

'Who is your mother? What is her name?'

'Claire.'

Claire was the English for Chiara. I thought for a second.

'Come with me, Allegra,' I said. 'We'll go downstairs.'

I wanted to show this little girl to Chiara. Then she would know that her daughter wasn't walking in her sleep – and *I* would know that I wasn't dreaming! I took the girl's cold little hand but she wouldn't come.

'No, no!' she cried in Italian again. 'My dear Mamà is at Bagno a Ripoli near Florence. I want to go there.'

I said, 'Wait here, Allegra. I'll go downstairs and bring my friend. She wants to see you. Wait here.'

I found Chiara in the long room. She was reading a book in an armchair by the fire. I told her that there was a girl in my room again. She looked surprised and followed me upstairs. We went along the corridor. My door was open and we went into the room. The child wasn't there.

We looked everywhere but found nothing. The only child in the house was Chiara's daughter.

'She's sleeping in her bed,' Chiara told me. 'Perhaps you had a dream, Adrian.'

'No, it wasn't a dream! There was a girl in my room a few minutes ago. I saw her and talked to her.'

Then I told Chiara everything about the girl. When I finished, she said:

'Well, it's very strange. Who is this girl? She isn't my daughter. My Allegra has got black hair and brown eyes. And my husband didn't take her away from me. I know that he wants to take her away, but he can't. Allegra lives with me. You see, I don't love my husband any more, and so he doesn't live here with us. He's in England. But Allegra likes him a lot and I know that she wants to see

We looked everywhere but found nothing.

him.' She was silent for a minute, then said, 'So the child in your room wants to see her mother, and Allegra wants to see her father. It's strange, isn't it? I don't understand it.'

Next day I went for a walk with Allegra Henderson. The big black dog came with us. We walked down a hill and came to a little river with a bridge. We stood on the bridge while Allegra dropped stones into the water and the dog tried to find them.

'Do you speak Italian, Allegra?' I asked.

'Oh yes! Listen.' And she spoke fast in Italian.

'Did you learn it at school?'

'Yes. It's a convent school and the teachers are Italian nuns. Look, Nero has got a stone in his mouth! Isn't he clever? Come here, Nero!'

'Allegra, do you know a place called Bagno a Ripoli?'

'No, I don't. Oh, don't shake the water over us, Nero – you bad boy!'

'Do you know anybody called Claire?'

'Yes, of course! That's Mummy's name in English.'

Allegra laughed. But she didn't laugh when I asked:

'Where's your Daddy, Allegra?'

She didn't answer me.

'You're a bad boy, Nero!' she said angrily. 'Give me that stone!'

I asked her the question again. This time she answered.

'Mummy says he's in England.'

Was she sad or angry? I didn't know.

'Do you want to see him?'

'Yes,' she said. And I saw that she was unhappy. She didn't want to talk about it.

'Why can't you see him?' I asked.

'Because Mummy says that he wants to take me away from her.'

'Would you like to go away with your Daddy?'

She looked at me for a second; then suddenly she began to cry.

'I want to see my Daddy!' she cried, sad and angry at the same time. 'I want to see him before I die! Why doesn't he come?'

And then she ran away. She ran fast up the hill and Nero ran behind her.

'I want to see him before I die! Why doesn't he come?'

My parents liked the villa so we stayed there for a week. But I wanted to go. I was afraid. Every night the blond Allegra came to my room in her long white nightdress, and asked me to take her to her Mamà. When I said no, she was always very angry with me.

And every day I talked and played with the dark-haired Allegra, Chiara's daughter. I liked her a lot and she liked me. We were good friends. But she was like two different people. Sometimes she spoke to me angrily, like the other Allegra in the night. At other times she was a happy, sweet little girl of five again. I often asked her why she thought that she was going to die. She always answered with the same words: 'I know, I know.'

During that week's holiday I began to feel love for Allegra Henderson. But there was the other Allegra who came at night. Who was she? I didn't believe in ghosts, but I was beginning to think that she *was* a ghost.

The day before we left, I wrote some notes:

ALLEGRA HENDERSON
- *5 years old. Tall, black hair, brown eyes, pale.*
- *Speaks English and Italian, but can't say 'r'.*
- *Mother's name Chiara. Calls her 'Mummy'.*
- *Wants to see her father, who lives in England.*
- *Thinks she is going to die.*

ALLEGRA THE GHOST
- *5 years old. Tall, blond hair, blue eyes, pale.*
- *Speaks English and Italian, but can't say 'r'.*
- *Mother's name Claire and lives at Bagno a Ripoli near Florence. Calls her 'Mamà'*
- *Wants to see her mother, but her father says no.*
- *Thinks she is going to die.*

I read these notes lots of times, but they didn't help me. Then I saw that I didn't know anything about the ghost Allegra's father. So I decided to ask her that night, which

'Papà is dead now.'

was our last night at the villa. I didn't sleep much that night; I waited and waited. But she didn't come. No, she didn't come and I was angry! I felt sure that her father was important.

Next morning we said goodbye to the Hendersons. When I said goodbye to Allegra, I felt sad. She was sad too, and she gave me a kiss.

'I hope that one day you will see your Daddy,' I said to her. 'Then you'll be happy.'

'Oh no,' she answered in a strange voice. 'Papà is dead now. He was a famous lord and he took me away from my Mamà. But he's dead now.'

We were all very surprised.

'What are you saying, Allegra?' Chiara said. 'Your father isn't a lord and he isn't dead! What a strange fantasy!'

But Allegra only smiled; a sad smile. And that was the last time I saw her.

3
Allegra Three

In England I went back to school and my studies, but I didn't forget Allegra. I wrote letters to her and sent some small presents. She didn't answer my letters but I said to myself, 'Well, she's only five. Perhaps she can't write letters yet.' Then a year after our holiday in Italy a letter arrived from Margaret Henderson. First she thanked me for my letters and presents. Then she wrote:

I'm sorry that we didn't write to you, but it has been a very bad year for us. It is difficult for me to write now, but today is April 21st and I want to tell you that something terrible happened on the same day last year. Chiara and I are still very sad, and Chiara has been ill. She doesn't eat much and she doesn't want to speak to anybody. Now I'll tell you why. A week after your holiday our little Allegra got a fever. A few days later the fever was worse and we called the doctor. He said that he wasn't sure what the fever was. 'Perhaps she drank some bad water or ate food that was bad,' he told us. He gave her some medicine and she was better. But then the fever returned very quickly. We couldn't find the doctor and when he arrived, it was too late. Our dear little Allegra died on April 21st a year ago. Oh, it's like a terrible dream! Our darling child was only five years and three months old. Now she has gone and she will never come back to us!

When I read this, I was shocked. Allegra dead! I felt very sad and I began to cry. For a long time I just couldn't believe it. I remembered her face, her voice, and her child's talk. I remembered our games and our conversations. Allegra came back to me like a ghost and I was very unhappy.

When I was eighteen, I went to university to study Italian, but I often remembered Allegra and that strange week at the Villa Henderson. How could I forget it? And I often thought about Allegra's strange words: 'I want to see my Daddy before I die.' How did she know that she was going to die? And then there was the ghost Allegra in my room, saying, 'I want to see my Mamà before I die.' What did it all mean? I wanted to find the answer to this mystery. But how?

In spring I went to Italy for my studies and I stayed in Florence with an Italian family. They had a little daughter. When they told me her name, I couldn't believe my ears.

'We wanted a different name,' the mother told me, 'a name that you don't often find in Italy. Allegra came to me suddenly. It's a beautiful name and we hoped that she would be a happy child. But she isn't happy. She's a strange girl.'

I looked at the child. She was tall; her face was pale and beautiful. She had long brown hair and brown eyes.

'How old is she?' I asked.

'She's five.'

'She isn't happy. She's a strange girl.'

'Five? Are you sure – I mean, is she?' I said, stupidly.

'Yes, five.' The mother looked at me strangely.

Can I ask you when she was five? I mean, when is her birthday?'

The mother looked surprised. 'In January. Why?'

'But please tell me the exact day. You see, I'd like to buy her a present next year.'

Now the mother was smiling. 'She was born on January 21st.'

When I went to my room that night, I was afraid and I didn't go to bed. I was thinking about Allegra Henderson. She died on April 21st when she was five years and three months old. So she was born on January 21st too! Was it possible that this Italian Allegra had the same name, the same birthday, the same age? I couldn't sleep so I tried to read a book about some English poets in Italy. But I couldn't. I was waiting, waiting . . .

She came at midnight. I looked at my watch and then she was there in a dark corner of the room. A beautiful, blond child, her skin like milk, her eyes like the blue of an Italian sky. She wore a long white nightdress. Allegra.

'Will you take me to my Mamà?' she asked in her beautiful English. 'She's at Bagno a Ripoli. It isn't far from here.'

I was very afraid now and I shouted, 'Go away! Go away!'

But she came and stood by my armchair.

'I want to see Mamà before I die. Take me!' she said angrily.

I ran out of that room very fast.

Next morning I decided to go to Bagno a Ripoli. I drove there in my small Fiat 500. There were only a few houses, and a small church called Santa Maria dell'Antella. I went into the church but there was nothing special about it. Then I walked around the small cemetery behind it. But I didn't see anything different so I decided to go back to Florence. When I was going out of the cemetery, I saw a tombstone with some English words on it. I stopped and read:

Here lies Claire Clairmont

Died in Florence

March 19th 1879

Aged 81

The name Claire again! The name of the ghost Allegra's mother! I was very surprised but I still didn't understand anything.

In Florence that afternoon I decided to go to a bar and read the book about the English poets. And while I was reading about Byron and Shelley, I began to understand the mystery of Allegra.

Here Lies
CLAIRE CLAIRMONT
Died in Florence
March 19th 1879
Aged 81

I saw a tombstone with some English words on it.

4
Lord Byron's daughter

This is what I read:

On January 21st 1817 Claire Clairmont, nineteen years old, had a baby daughter in a town called Bath in England. The baby's father was the poet Lord Byron, but he was not Claire's husband. They were lovers for a while but then Byron went to Italy. He did not love Claire and he did not want to be with her. So Claire lived with Byron's friends – the poet Shelley, his wife Mary, and their two children. Claire and Mary were half-sisters; they had the same father but different mothers. Shelley liked children very much and he felt a strong love for Claire's baby. He hoped that his friend Byron would help Claire and her daughter. From Bath he wrote to him:

Claire has a very beautiful girl. Her hair is fair and her eyes are blue . . . Claire calls her Alba.

Byron wanted to see his baby daughter and he asked Shelley to bring her to Italy. Shelley wanted to live in Italy too, so he and his family, and Claire and her baby, all travelled there. The baby was a year old and now she was called Allegra because Byron liked the name.

In Italy Claire decided to give Allegra to Byron because

she thought that the daughter of an English lord would have a good future. Shelley said to her: 'No, don't do it, Claire, or you will never see your daughter again.' But Byron was rich and Claire thought that Allegra would have a better life with him. Of course, she did not *want* to give Allegra to Byron, and when she sent the child to him in Venice, she was very unhappy. In a letter to a friend she wrote:

In the spring of 1818 I sent my little darling to her father. She was the only thing that I loved in the world.

It was a terrible mistake. Allegra lived with her father in a big house called the Palazzo Mocenigo. It was full of strange animals, and even stranger people. After a while Lord Byron understood that it was not a good home for a child. So he gave Allegra to an English family in Venice, and in August Claire saw her there. Then Byron said that Claire and her baby and Shelley's family could stay at his villa near a town called Este. For two months Claire was happy there with Allegra. But Byron also said that she must bring Allegra to him in Venice in the autumn. So in October Allegra went back to her father, and Claire never saw her again.

Allegra stayed in Venice for eight months with different families. Then Byron took her to the city of

The house was full of strange animals, and even stranger people.

Bologna. He wrote to Shelley:

She is like me. She has white skin. Her voice is soft and she can't say the letter 'r'.

For many months he sent no news to Claire about her daughter. Then she heard that Allegra was with her father in a town called Ravenna. She wrote to him, 'I want to see my daughter – please!' But he said no. Claire wrote a lot of letters like this to Byron, but he did

not answer them. She was very unhappy.

When Allegra was four years old, Byron sent her to a convent school near Ravenna. The nuns were kind and loved her very much. But the convent was strange to her. The walls were white and cold, the rooms were empty, and sometimes she was cold because there was no fire. Every day she did the same things at the same time. This quiet life was very different from her life with Byron.

Claire was now very angry. She did not like convent schools, and she was sure that Allegra was always cold and lonely. She wrote an angry letter to Byron: 'My child must be with one of her parents,' she said. He did not answer the letter. He thought that the convent was good for Allegra, and he told the nuns that Claire must never visit the child. They must lock the doors to stop her. But he said that Shelley could see Allegra because he was his friend. So one day Shelley went to visit Allegra at the convent. He wrote in his diary:

She is tall and pale. But her eyes are very blue, and she has a lot of blond hair. She is beautiful and very different from the other children. I ran and played with her in the garden. She is very light and fast. I gave her some sweets and I asked her, 'What shall I say to your Mamà?' She answered in Italian, 'Tell her to send me a kiss and a beautiful dress.' Then I asked her, 'What shall I say to your Papà?' And she answered, 'Tell him to visit me and to bring Mamà with him.'

But Papà did not visit her and Mamà did not come.

On June 6th 1821 Claire dreamt that Allegra was ill. She thought that her daughter was going to die and she would never see her again. 'Take her away from the convent,' she wrote to Byron. But he said no. Of course,

Shelley went to visit Allegra at the convent.

Claire wanted to go to the convent and take Allegra away, but this was very difficult. Byron was a rich and famous lord and the people in the convent did what he wanted. They locked the doors.

And then Allegra got a fever. The doctor came and gave her some medicine. For a while she was better and the nuns hoped that she would live. But she died on April 21st 1822. She was five years and three months old.

Shelley was afraid to tell Claire that Allegra was dead. He thought that she would try to kill herself. But one evening Shelley, Mary, and some friends were talking about Allegra when Claire came into the room. At once everybody stopped talking, and she knew.

'Allegra's dead, isn't she?' she said.

So Shelley told her the sad story. She was very unhappy and wanted to die. Shelley was also unhappy. He loved Allegra like a daughter and he could not forget her. Two weeks after Allegra died, he was with one of his friends on the balcony of a house by the sea. Suddenly he saw a child with long, fair hair and very blue eyes. She was coming out of the sea and she was smiling at him. In the moonlight he saw that she wanted to come to him.

'Look, there it is!' he said to his friend. 'Can you see her? Look – there!'

But his friend saw nothing. It was Allegra's ghost.

And fifty years after Allegra died, Claire wrote to a friend:

I can never forget my darling child. But did she really die? Byron and Shelley said that she died, but I have heard that she is alive. Some people say that they have seen her. I am sure that she is alive.

Claire died in 1879 when she was eighty-one years old. Her tombstone is in the cemetery of Santa Maria dell'Antella at Bagno a Ripoli.

Shelley told Claire the sad story.

5
Bagno a Ripoli

After I read this strange, sad story, I understood the mystery of Allegra. Was she still alive? No. But her ghost was still in the world. The little girl in my room was the ghost of Claire Clairmont's Allegra. She was unhappy and she couldn't rest because she wanted to be with her mother. But she couldn't find her. She knew that her mother was at Bagno a Ripoli, but she didn't know how to get there. So her unhappy ghost lived and waited in the body of Allegra Henderson, Chiara's daughter. At night it left Allegra's body and came to my room for help. Then poor Allegra died of fever, just like Claire's Allegra. But the ghost couldn't rest; it had to find another child's body.

'Who is the child?' I asked myself. 'Who is the next Allegra – Allegra Three?'

But I already knew the answer. My Italian family in Florence had a little daughter. Her name was Allegra, and she would be five years and three months on April 21st.

It was now the evening of April 20th.

I left the bar quickly and ran back to my family's house. When I arrived, the mother was crying.

'Allegra is in hospital,' she told me. 'She's got a bad fever and the doctors aren't sure what it is. Oh, I hope it isn't dangerous! I hope she'll get better soon!'

'Allegra is in hospital,' she told me.

'She'll be all right," I said. 'She'll get better.'

But that night in my room I said to myself, 'Oh, please – no, no!'

I walked round and round the room and I thought of my dear friend Allegra Henderson. I was afraid that Allegra Three was going to die the next day. But what could I do about it?

'No! This Allegra must not die!' I said angrily.

Then, suddenly, I knew what to do. I waited. Ten o'clock, eleven o'clock, midnight. 'Please, please, come!' I said.

I looked at my watch. Twelve fifteen.

'Will she come, will she come?' I said again and again.

And then she was there: the ghost of Lord Byron's daughter! Pale, beautiful, with big blue eyes and hair like gold. She was smiling at me.

'Are you going to take me to Mamà?'

'Yes, Allegra. We're going to Bagno a Ripoli. But we must hurry. Come on, let's go!'

She laughed happily. 'Oh, thank you! You're so kind!'

I took her cold little hand. We went out of the house and got into my car. I drove very fast through the night.

'Oh, I'm going to see my dear Mamà!' Allegra said. 'I'll be with her after all these years. We'll be so happy! I loved her and she loved me. But Papà took me away from

I took her to Claire Clairmont's tombstone.

her and he sent me to a convent school. I didn't like it there. It was so cold and quiet! Mamà didn't come and Papà didn't come. Why didn't they come?'

But then she laughed and began to sing an Italian song.

When we arrived at Bagno a Ripoli, she jumped out of the car and looked around.

'Where is Mamà?' she cried.

'Follow me,' I said.

We went into the cemetery and I took her to Claire Clairmont's tombstone.

'She's here,' I said. 'Your Mamà is here.'

Allegra read the name on the tombstone.

'Mamà?' she called. 'Are you here? It's me, Allegra. I'm here, your Allegra is here.' She was crying with happiness.

I was happy too, but I was also afraid. The cemetery was dark and silent, there was a soft wind in the trees, and in front of my eyes was this little child's ghost in a white nightdress, calling for its dead mother.

'Yes, I hear you, Mamà!' Allegra cried. 'I'm coming, I'm coming . . .'

And very slowly the ghost of Allegra began to disappear. And her voice was slowly going away.

'Wait for me, Mamà! I'm coming . . . I'm coming . . .'

And then the ghost wasn't there. Allegra was with her mother at last.

6
Allegra Four

At eight o'clock the next morning Allegra's mother came to my room and woke me up. She had a big smile on her face.

'My Allegra is much better!' she said. 'The doctor telephoned early this morning. He says that the fever has gone. It went suddenly last night. She's going to get well. Oh, I'm so happy! I'm going to the hospital to bring her home. Would you like to come with me?'

So we went to the hospital and I saw Allegra. She looked a little tired but she was well. Perhaps you can understand how I felt. Allegra Henderson was dead – but I felt that she was alive again!

That was on April 21st, eight years ago.

And now? Well, six years ago I met an Italian girl and we fell in love. We got married and a year later my wife had a baby girl. She's got long black hair and green eyes. Her face is pale but beautiful. She is tall for her years. She speaks English and Italian very well, but she can't say 'r'. Yes, she's like my little friend Allegra who died twelve years ago. But she's a happy child.

She's like my little friend Allegra who died twelve years ago.

Today I've asked her lots of times, 'How are you? Do you feel well?'

'Yes, Daddy, of course I feel well,' she says. And she laughs.

'Are you sure?'

'Yes! I feel fine. Why?'

But I don't want to tell her why. You see, today is April 20th and tomorrow my daughter will be five years and three months old.

Oh! I forgot to tell you her name! But you know it already – don't you?

GLOSSARY

age   the number of years that a person has lived

balcony   a place on the outside wall of a building above the ground, where you can stand or sit

bar   a room where people can buy and have drinks

believe   to think that something is true or possible

blond   with a light colour

cemetery   a place where dead people are put under the ground

convent   a building where nuns live and work (see 'nun')

corridor   a long narrow passage inside a building

curtain   a piece of material in front of a window

darling   a word for someone that you love very much

disappear   to go away where nobody can see you

dream *(n)*   a picture in the mind when you are sleeping

fair   with a light colour

fantasy   a wild, strange idea that cannot be true or real

fever   an illness when your body feels burning hot

future   the time that is coming

ghost   the spirit of a dead person, which looks real but perhaps isn't real

kiss *(n)*   a touch with the lips to show love

lord   a man from a rich, noble family

lover   somebody who makes love with another person

medicine   something special to eat or drink that helps a person who is ill to get better

nun   a woman who lives to serve Jesus Christ

pale   with very little colour in the face

poet   a person who writes poems

sad   not happy

shocked   very surprised, by something bad or terrible

shutter   a cover for a window on the wall outside a building

sign *(n)*   (here) a piece of wood or metal by the road that gives you information about something

skin   the thin covering on the outside of a body

tombstone   a stone in a cemetery, with the name of the dead person on it

university   a place where people go to study after they leave school

The Mystery of Allegra

ACTIVITIES

Before Reading

1 Read the back cover. How much do you know now about *The Mystery of Allegra*? Tick one box for each sentence.

	YES	NO
1 There are two girls called Allegra.	☐	☐
2 The name 'Allegra' means 'happy'.	☐	☐
3 The first Allegra is ten years old.	☐	☐
4 She is never unhappy.	☐	☐
5 She has a friend called Adrian.	☐	☐
6 The second Allegra is there every morning.	☐	☐
7 She has cold hands and a cold face.	☐	☐

2 Read the story introduction on the first page of the book. What is going to happen in the story? Can you guess? Tick one box for each sentence.

	YES	NO
1 A girl called Allegra will die.	☐	☐
2 Adrian will be in danger.	☐	☐
3 Adrian will help a girl called Allegra.	☐	☐
4 A girl called Allegra will kill somebody.	☐	☐
5 Adrian will find out that the second Allegra is not a real person.	☐	☐
6 There will be four girls called Allegra in this story.	☐	☐

While Reading

**Read Chapter 1. Are these sentences true (T) or false (F)?
Rewrite the false ones with the correct information.**

1 Adrian met Allegra twelve years ago.
2 Adrian and his parents were on holiday in France.
3 Margaret Henderson was Italian.
4 Margaret had a daughter and a granddaughter.
5 Adrian didn't wake up in the night.
6 A little girl came into Adrian's room in the night.
7 Allegra said that her mother was in the house.
8 Adrian didn't see how Allegra left his room.
9 Adrian didn't see anybody in the next bedroom.
10 Chiara said that Allegra sometimes walked in her sleep.

**Read Chapter 2. Choose the best question-word for these
questions and then answer them.**

Who / Where

1 . . . had long black hair and brown eyes?
2 . . . couldn't go to sleep at first because he was afraid?
3 . . . did Allegra want to go?
4 . . . did Chiara's husband live?
5 . . . wanted to see her father?
6 . . . wanted to see her mother?

Read Chapter 3, then answer these questions.

1 Why didn't Allegra answer Adrian's letters?
2 How old was Allegra when she died?
3 Why did Adrian go to Florence?
4 Who had the same name and birthday as Allegra Henderson?
5 Who came to Adrian's room at midnight?
6 Where did Adrian go the next morning?
7 When and where did Claire Clairmont die?

Before you read Chapter 4, what can you guess about the mystery of Allegra? Choose Y (Yes) or N (No) for each sentence.

1 Claire Clairmont had a daughter called Allegra. Y/N
2 Claire Clairmont's daughter died when she was five. Y/N
3 The first Allegra's father was an English poet. Y/N
4 Claire Clairmont didn't love her daughter. Y/N
5 Allegra was living with her father when she died. Y/N
6 Adrian was the only person who ever saw the ghost of Allegra. Y/N

Read Chapter 4 and check your guesses. Then answer these questions.

1 What was Allegra's father's name?
2 Who chose the name Allegra?

3 Why did Claire give Allegra to her father?
4 Where did Byron send Allegra when she was four?
5 Who went to visit Allegra?

Read Chapter 5. Who said this, and to whom?

1 'Allegra is in hospital.'
2 'She'll get better.'
3 'We're going to Bagno a Ripoli.'
4 'Where is Mamà?'
5 'I'm here, your Allegra is here.'

Read Chapter 6. Here are some untrue sentences. Rewrite them with the correct information.

1 The doctor said that the third Allegra was going to die.
2 Adrian married an English girl.
3 Adrian and his wife had a baby boy.
4 Adrian's child doesn't speak English.
5 Adrian's daughter is an unhappy child.

Now answer these questions.

1 What is Adrian's daughter's name?
2 When is her birthday?
3 Is she going to die on April 21st?

After Reading

1 **Match these halves of sentences to explain the mystery of Allegra. Use these words to join your sentences.**

and / and / because / but / but / but / when

1 Claire Clairmont's daughter, Allegra, died in 1822,

   _____

2 She was unhappy _____

3 She wanted to go to Bagno a Ripoli _____

4 So she came to Adrian's room at night _____

5 _____ Allegra Henderson died,

6 Then the third Allegra became ill too, _____

7 He took the ghost Allegra to Bagno a Ripoli _____

8 she wanted to be with her mother.

9 she found her mother there.

10 asked him for help.

11 the ghost went to live in the body of the Italian family's Allegra.

12 her ghost lived in the body of Allegra Henderson.

13 Adrian knew how to help her.

14 she couldn't get there alone.

2 **Read this description of Allegra One. Then write similar descriptions of Allegra Two, Allegra Three, and Allegra Four. Make any changes that are necessary.**

Claire Clairmont's daughter was called Allegra, but she was often sad. She was tall and pale and she had big blue eyes and long blond hair. She could speak English and Italian but she couldn't say the letter 'r'. She was born on January 21st and she died on April 21st, when she was five years old.

3 **Imagine that in June 1821 Claire went to see Byron and asked to see Allegra. Complete their conversation. Use as many words as you like.**

CLAIRE: You must let me see Allegra. Why did you send her to that terrible convent school?

BYRON: Because _____.

CLAIRE: No, it isn't. I'm sure that _____. I'm going to take her away.

BYRON: Well, you can't. I've told the nuns _____.

CLAIRE: You're so unkind. I'm Allegra's mother. And I know that she's ill.

BYRON: How _____?

CLAIRE: I _____. I think that she's going to die.

BYRON: Of course she _____.

CLAIRE: You don't love her. You don't want her with you, so why _____?

BYRON: Because she must _____.

4 Here is a new illustration for the story. Find the best place in the story to put the picture, and answer these questions.

The picture goes on page _____.

1 Who are the two people in the picture?
2 Where are they going?
3 Why?

Now write a caption for the illustration.

Caption: _____

5 **Do you agree (A) or disagree (D) with these sentences? Explain why.**

1 Claire Clairmont was wrong to give Allegra to Byron.
2 Byron was a very bad father.
3 Chiara Henderson was wrong to take her daughter to Italy when her husband still lived in England.
4 It was dangerous for Adrian to call his daughter Allegra.
5 Allegra One wasn't a ghost; she was just Adrian's dream.

6 **Fill in the gaps in this text about ghosts. Use these words.**

afraid, cold, dead, locked, night, rest, room, see, unhappy, wear

They say that ghosts are _____ people who cannot _____. They are usually _____. Ghosts come at _____; they often _____ white clothes, and they are _____ when you touch them. They can come into a _____ when the door and windows are _____. When they leave, you don't _____ where they go. People are often _____ of ghosts.

7 **Now discuss your answers to these questions.**

1 Do you believe in ghosts?
2 Have you or any of your friends ever seen a ghost?
3 Have you seen any films or TV programmes about ghosts?
4 Would you like to see a ghost? Why or why not?

ABOUT THE AUTHOR

Peter Foreman has worked in English Language Teaching for twenty-five years, and has taught mostly in Italy, but also in Spain and Greece. He lived in Italy for many years, and has published two holiday books and several books of short fiction for students of English. He now lives and works near Bath, in the west of England. *The Mystery of Allegra* is his first story for the Oxford Bookworms Library.

The idea for this story came to him one weekend, when he was staying in a guest house in Tuscany. There were two English women there and one of their daughters was called Allegra. He remembered that this beautiful and unusual name was also the name of Byron's daughter, who died very young. He has never seen a ghost himself, but he began to imagine the ghost of Byron's Allegra, looking for her mother . . .

OXFORD BOOKWORMS LIBRARY

Classics • Crime & Mystery • Factfiles • Fantasy & Horror
Human Interest • Playscripts • Thriller & Adventure
True Stories • World Stories

The OXFORD BOOKWORMS LIBRARY provides enjoyable reading in English, with a wide range of classic and modern fiction, non-fiction, and plays. It includes original and adapted texts in seven carefully graded language stages, which take learners from beginner to advanced level. An overview is given on the next pages.

All Stage 1 titles are available as audio recordings, as well as over eighty other titles from Starter to Stage 6. All Starters and many titles at Stages 1 to 4 are specially recommended for younger learners. Every Bookworm is illustrated, and Starters and Factfiles have full-colour illustrations.

The OXFORD BOOKWORMS LIBRARY also offers extensive support. Each book contains an introduction to the story, notes about the author, a glossary, and activities. Additional resources include tests and worksheets, and answers for these and for the activities in the books. There is advice on running a class library, using audio recordings, and the many ways of using Oxford Bookworms in reading programmes. Resource materials are available on the website <www.oup.com/bookworms>.

The *Oxford Bookworms Collection* is a series for advanced learners. It consists of volumes of short stories by well-known authors, both classic and modern. Texts are not abridged or adapted in any way, but carefully selected to be accessible to the advanced student.

You can find details and a full list of titles in the *Oxford Bookworms Library Catalogue* and *Oxford English Language Teaching Catalogues*, and on the website <www.oup.com/bookworms>.

THE OXFORD BOOKWORMS LIBRARY
GRADING AND SAMPLE EXTRACTS

STARTER • 250 HEADWORDS

present simple – present continuous – imperative –
can/cannot, *must* – *going to* (future) – simple gerunds …

Her phone is ringing – but where is it?

Sally gets out of bed and looks in her bag. No phone. She looks under the bed. No phone. Then she looks behind the door. There is her phone. Sally picks up her phone and answers it. *Sally's Phone*

STAGE 1 • 400 HEADWORDS

… past simple – coordination with *and, but, or* –
subordination with *before, after, when, because, so* …

I knew him in Persia. He was a famous builder and I worked with him there. For a time I was his friend, but not for long. When he came to Paris, I came after him – I wanted to watch him. He was a very clever, very dangerous man. *The Phantom of the Opera*

STAGE 2 • 700 HEADWORDS

… present perfect – *will* (future) – *(don't) have to, must not, could* –
comparison of adjectives – simple *if* clauses – past continuous –
tag questions – *ask/tell* + infinitive …

While I was writing these words in my diary, I decided what to do. I must try to escape. I shall try to get down the wall outside. The window is high above the ground, but I have to try. I shall take some of the gold with me – if I escape, perhaps it will be helpful later. *Dracula*

STAGE 3 • 1000 HEADWORDS

... should, may – present perfect continuous – *used to* – past perfect –
causative – relative clauses – indirect statements ...

Of course, it was most important that no one should see
Colin, Mary, or Dickon entering the secret garden. So Colin
gave orders to the gardeners that they must all keep away
from that part of the garden in future. *The Secret Garden*

STAGE 4 • 1400 HEADWORDS

*... past perfect continuous – passive (simple forms) –
would* conditional clauses – indirect questions –
relatives with *where/when* – gerunds after prepositions/phrases ...

I was glad. Now Hyde could not show his face to the world
again. If he did, every honest man in London would be
proud to report him to the police. *Dr Jekyll and Mr Hyde*

STAGE 5 • 1800 HEADWORDS

*... future continuous – future perfect –
passive (modals, continuous forms) –
would have* conditional clauses – modals + perfect infinitive ...

If he had spoken Estella's name, I would have hit him. I was
so angry with him, and so depressed about my future, that I
could not eat the breakfast. Instead I went straight to the old
house. *Great Expectations*

STAGE 6 • 2500 HEADWORDS

*... passive (infinitives, gerunds) – advanced modal meanings –
clauses of concession, condition*

When I stepped up to the piano, I was confident. It was as if I
knew that the prodigy side of me really did exist. And when
I started to play, I was so caught up in how lovely I looked
that I didn't worry how I would sound. *The Joy Luck Club*

BOOKWORMS • FANTASY & HORROR • STAGE 2

The Pit and the Pendulum and Other Stories

EDGAR ALLAN POE

Retold by John Escott

Everybody has bad dreams, when horrible things move towards you in the dark, things you can hear but not see. Then you wake up, in your own warm bed, and turn over to go back to sleep.

But suppose you wake up on a hard prison floor, in a darkness blacker than the blackest night. You hear the sound of water, you touch a cold metal wall, and smell a wet dead smell. Death is all around you, waiting . . .

In these stories by Edgar Allan Poe, death whispers at you from every dark corner, and fear can drive you mad . . .

BOOKWORMS • TRUE STORIES • STAGE 2

The Death of Karen Silkwood

JOYCE HANNAM

This is the story of Karen Silkwood. It begins with her death.

Why does her story begin where it should end? Certain people wanted her death to be an ending. Why? What were they afraid of? Karen Silkwood had something to tell us, and she believed that it was important. Why didn't she live to tell us? Will we ever know what really happened? The questions go on and on, but there are no answers.

This is a true story. It happened in Oklahoma, USA, where Karen Silkwood lived and worked . . . and died.